Printed in Great Britain. For information address Harper & Row, Publishers, Inc., 10 East 53rd Street, New York, N.Y. 10022.

Library of Congress Catalog Card Number: 77-5218
Trade ISBN 0-06-022224-7
Harpercrest ISBN 0-06-022225-5

First American Edition

Printed in Great Britain by Cox and Wyman Ltd, London, Reading and Fakenham

Anita Harper and Christine Roche are both members of the Kids' Book Group, a collective of women writers and illustrators.

How We Work

by Anita Harper
with pictures by Christine Roche
of the Kids' Book Group

Harper & Row, Publishers
New York, Hagerstown, San Francisco, London

People work at all kinds of jobs.

Some people work together.

Some people work alone.

Some people work high up.

Some people work low down.

Some people work
while others sleep.

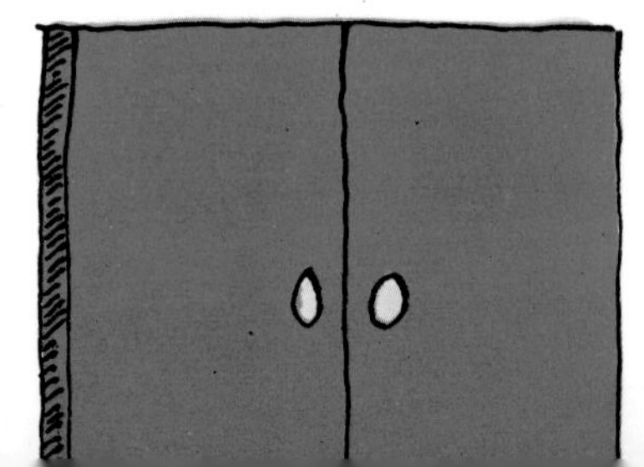

Some people sleep while others work.

Some people like their work.

Some people find it boring.

Some people have one job.

Some people have more than one job.

Some people work long hours.

Some people work short hours.

Some people get paid a lot for what they do.

Some people get paid very little.

Some people can find no work.

1+3=2
2+1=

Some people work
and don't get paid at all.

People work all over the world.